LIVING RESTFULLY

A Skeptic's Guide to Raising Children Screen-Free

Tamara McLeod Harper

Living Restfully: A Skeptic's Guide to Raising Children Screen-Free

ISBN-13: 978-1500971069

Cover Illustrations by Nikki Kintner
Cover Design & Layout by Tamara Harper
Edited by Melissa Hall

Scripture quotations are from The Holy Bible, English Standard Version (ESV), copyright © 2001 by Crossway, a publishing ministry of Good News Publishers. Used by permission. All rights reserved.

Portions of "Setting to Sea in the Leaky Boat of Self (Upadana)" by Akincano Marc Weber, used with permission. http://dharmaseed.org/teacher/360/talk/24014/ Licensed under CC BY-NC-ND 3.0

Illustrations for Cycle of Restlessness in Chapter One by Tamara Harper.

Graph in Chapter Two used with permission. Sigman, Aric. "Well Connected?" *The Biologist* Vol 59 No 1 (2009): 15

Harper family portrait used with permission. Original artwork by Chris Garrison.

Author has no control over, and assumes no responsibility for, the content, privacy policies, or practices of any websites referenced in this work.

For parents who feel run down by the routine of their home,

For children who are restless, unable to lose themselves in imaginary play for hours on end,

For families who are struggling to find a balance of appropriate screen time.

CONTENTS

INTRODUCTION

Raising children is hard. My husband, Jamie, and I have two young children. For years, on any given day, I felt stretched to exhaustion by work, chores, and most of all the kids' daily demands. Our family still has plenty of room to grow, but over the last several months, we have experienced major positive transformations. In hopes that others might benefit from the lessons I learned working through my stubborn pride, I am happy to share our story.

For too long, our kids were stuck in what I call "the cycle of restlessness." *Restlessness* is my go-to word for my children's continual neediness and whining. I never really knew how to handle restlessness. Sometimes, I fought against it with a passion: I reprimanded them for it, I punished them for it, and I grew tired of it. Other times, to keep my sanity, I accepted their behavior as normal. I convinced myself that it was a phase. Jamie and I addressed the kids' restlessness one day at a time. We tried adjusting our parenting methods, shifting discipline strategies, monitoring sugar intake, moving bedtime up—nothing seemed to help.

Then, we became suspicious of the effects of screen time on our children's behavior. I use the term *screen time* in reference to using smartphones, tablets, televisions, computer games, movies, video games, handheld devices, portable DVD players, and the like. As I began researching screen time effects on children, I started to reconsider my family's screen time routines.

When we took a step back, Jamie and I could see that our kids were a bit obsessed with screens, but this was difficult for me to admit. I was proud of the fact that we had always put limits on screen time in our home. Our general rule of thumb was an hour or less per day. App time on our phones or Netflix time in the afternoon was both exciting for the kids and comforting to me. Kicking my beloved screen time parenting crutch was absolutely *the last thing* that I was willing to try. But, finally, begrudgingly, desperately, we took the plunge: we would create a screen-free home life for our kids.

To our family, *screen-free* refers to two things at once: a *mindset* that is liberated from the lure of screens, and a *routine* that avoids the regular use of screens, unless reasonably necessary or uniquely useful. Much to my surprise, the transition wasn't at all as difficult as I anticipated. It was a rough ride for several days, to be sure. But only for several days—not months, not weeks. The difficulties did not have the intensity or the longevity I had initially feared, and the benefits have been greater and more numerous than I ever anticipated.

As the kids gave up their obsession with screens, their restlessness began fading away. Jamie and I were greatly encouraged. However, we began to realize that their obsessive habit had actually *shifted*—away from screens and on to new *stuff*: toys, books, Lego sets, board games. And just as I was proud of our initial screen-time limits, Jamie and I have always been intentional about modeling simplicity in our home. So, the kids' sudden greed for acquiring new things was confounding. I wondered anew, *What is going on with their behavior?*

As Christian parents, Jamie and I feel a particular responsibility to teach our children that only God is worth our obsession—our worship. If we are not a slave to one thing, we are a slave to another. In a sense, restlessness is evidence of a need for God's grace. So, while Jamie and I try to manage the kids' exposure to screens, to new "stuff," junk food, places to go, and everything else that vies for their attention, we are joyfully compelled to point them to Jesus.

I've seen many children, like mine, who live in a continual state of restlessness because of an addiction to screen time. For our children's generation, screen time is arguably most powerful force grappling for their attention. As parents, we need to acknowledge the risks of allowing too much screen time and set boundaries for the health of our children. It may seem overwhelming or impossible to give up kids' screen time at home, but there are simple ways that we can create a healthy environment for our children to thrive: physically, mentally, and spiritually. I hope that my family's story will be a source of encouragement, inspiration, and empowerment for you and your family.

Chapter One

THE ROUTINE

Miserable Moderation

"Mama, what should we dooooo?"

"What is it *time* for?"

"I'm borrrrred..."

"What can I playyyyy?"

"After this, I wanna do something *funnn*."

"This is just taking so long . . ."

"I need a snaaaaack."

My kids have been restless all day. I'm at home with my five-year-old son, Isaiah, and my two-year-old daughter, Ellie. I'm a part-time music teacher, and otherwise I stay home with my beautiful, demanding, wound-up children. They have worn me out, and my sweet husband, Jamie, won't be home for an hour.

Home should be a place where you can rest . . . right? Why does it feel like I have to fight for rest day in and day out?

The sink is full of dirty dishes, the fridge is empty, and it will be dinner time soon. There are random items and toys strewn around the floor. The kids' complaints start up again. I take a deep breath. It's time to hit the brakes. I'm tired, but not without hope. My spiritual, eternal hope is in Jesus. Jamie and I pray and try our best to teach our children that He loves us more than we know. We try to model God's love in our home—we can depend on Him in any circumstance. At moments like these, I pray in desperation.

Utilizing what little energy I have left for them, I plead, "Kids! Please calm down. Let's remember self-control, ok?"

They do not respond much to this, and I am stretched to my limit. I need a crutch. I always have the option of an easy out, if I need it. I know how to buy myself 24 minutes of sanity: with *Dora the Explorer*. With minimal effort on my part, I'm able to milk this moment for all its worth. It's a balancing act of dangling the carrot while issuing tiny threats and demands.

I shrug my shoulders and say, "As soon as you calm down and straighten up, maybe we could watch Dora . . ."

Now the kids respond. They pick toys off of the floor, promise good behavior, and sit on the couch with hands folded. They prove themselves worthy of TV time. All in all, that initial moment of disaster transforms into a moment of peace.

And at this point, I should start dinner, but I need a *minute*. I turn on the tube and toss some fruit snacks to the kids—because, like clockwork, they will "need a snaaaack" in about three minutes. I sneak away to lie down and scan my Facebook feed. Bleary-eyed, I pause at an article[1] titled, "10 Reasons Handheld Devices Should Be Banned for Children Under the Age of 12."

I think, *Ok, I am an educated person. I've read that kids under two years old shouldn't have screen time. But when my kids were that young, I couldn't figure out how to get a shower without popping in a Baby Einstein video. They seem to be doing alright.*

Wait, did that say 12 years old? (Eye roll.) Everything in moderation, people! Screens are just tools that can be used for many purposes—many of them educational. And it's inevitable that they'll need those skills down the road, so it's probably all the better that they learn how to use them early on!

Plus, we don't even have cable, so I'm not exposing my kids to advertisements! And sure, every once in a while, we will allow them to play games on our smartphones, but we cut them off after a while. And video games? We just have the Wii and PBSKids.org. If they misbehave, they could lose it all. They know that. We've even gone a whole week without TV before! We have boundaries! We have balance! Not a big deal.

So, we were living (I believed) the balanced life of moderate screen time. Jamie and I modeled it as adults, and we insisted on it in our parenting.

Yet, in the midst of my kids' restlessness, in the 24-minutes-at-a-time sanity, in my self-affirmation of parenting preferences, and in my daily exhaustion, I never wanted to admit that I was slightly miserable. Because, I basically have it made. Jamie is the most supportive husband in the world. Our parents live in town. We have a strong community of friends. So, I couldn't understand why I was struggling so much. I felt like a weak wife for my strong husband. A frazzled mother for my smart, beautiful kids.

More and more, the kids were wearing me down with their constant need for entertainment and attention. And obviously, all children need attention from their parents. Quality time is a vital part of a child's basic needs. However, the incessant whining, complaining, fidgeting—the *restlessness*—left me struggling for control. My kids were driving me to mental exhaustion every day, and I couldn't handle it anymore. Perhaps the one bright spot in my prideful parenting was that I refused to believe that I was powerless to stop it.

My Good Intentions and Close-Mindedness

I wasn't sure where to start in making changes to combat restlessness in my home, but I was willing to try *almost* anything. I began to consider what practical steps we could take in our daily routines.

Adjust our diet? Less high-fructose corn syrup?

Spend more time outside?

Shift discipline strategies?

Be more hands-off?

Be more hands-on?

Take away screens?

Ha, I thought. *Like that article was talking about. Take it away until they're 12 years old. That would absolutely be the last thing that I would try! Taking TV away is a punishment for them, but it's also a punishment for me. It's so much harder when they can't watch it. But we've survived an entire week without it, so I know that can't be the real problem. For them to go without it, for years? I mean, there's just no reason! I can't even imagine. There may be some benefits for a while, but in the long run, it's not a big deal.*

In my mind, taking away screens from my children was simply not a viable option.

It took some time for me to hear myself. But when I finally acknowledged that, seriously, bottom line, I felt that I *needed* to hold on to screens "in moderation!" as a convenient parenting crutch, one that I *couldn't even imagine* completely letting it go—I started to see a red flag in my perspective: my mind was completely closed to removing screens from our children's home life.

Waking Up

I was sitting at the kitchen table one morning, drinking coffee and thinking through my to-do list, when Ellie, my two-year-old, proudly walks up and says, "Here's your phone, Mama!" She has my smartphone in her hand and gives it to me.

I freeze. The simple gesture feels jarring, significant.

I slowly say, "That's right. This *is* my phone—thank you! But I don't need it right now." I demonstrate this by putting it face down on the table.

As Ellie toddles away, I imagine her years from now, as a college student, chatting with her roommates, musing about growing up, about life issues, commenting, "Yeah. My mom was *always* on her phone. I mean, she had it with her *all the time*."

The image sticks with me the rest of the day. I try to shake it. *I'm overreacting. That is not going to happen—I'm modeling screen-time moderation for my kids! It's a daily part of my life. And that's normal. And for my child to notice indicates how smart she is—not that she thinks that I need it all the time or that I'm distracted. Anyway, I would never get my emails done if it weren't for the phone. Our schedule is so hectic, most days, I feel like I'm just getting by! Some days, my only accomplishment is that I kept the kids alive!*

On the one hand, I felt justified in our screen-time habits. The kids enjoyed their smartphone apps time, a little computer time, some educational programming, a few kids' TV shows, a couple of video games on the Wii—not all of this every day, just a little here and there. My kids weren't under the age of two anymore, and screens are not a big deal in small doses, right?

On the other hand, I couldn't ignore a nagging curiosity, a growing concern, and eventually a personal conviction about the negative influence screen time was having on my family.

As my denial diminished to make way for concern, I started analyzing the power of screens in our home. I observed the kids' behavior in relation to how much screen time they had. I kept my own screen habits in check. Together, Jamie and I made it a point to discuss screen time and its apparent effects on our family. The more that we analyzed the power of all of those screens in our home, the more concerned we became. We began to observe, what I call "the cycle of restlessness."

The Cycle of Restlessness

Daily Screen Habit

Child is blissfully sucked into screens on a daily basis. Characteristics include wide-eyed staring, tunnel vision, and perhaps a bit of drool and heavy breathing.

Increasingly Intense Anticipation

Child becomes more and more concerned about whether it is screen time yet. Characteristics include anxiety, whining, fidgeting, and that panicked look in her eye.

Full-Blown Addiction

Child is completely obsessed with screens. Characteristics include loss of self-control and screaming. The parent may have the urge to mimic these traits; however, that is not recommended.

Discipline

Parent puts into place stricter screen-time limits as punishment for child's bad behavior. Screen time "privileges" are then re-instated, as soon as they are "deserved."

Daily Screen Habit

Back to square one: the cycle begins again . . . with no end in sight.

Here's how the cycle played out in each of our children:

First, there was our two-year-old. Within the supposed safety of screen-time moderation, I couldn't understand why Ellie was becoming a TV addict. Our weekday routine looked something like this: drop Isaiah off at school, run a quick errand or two, maybe go to the gym. Then we would have some downtime at home, eat lunch, and then school carpool in the afternoon.

Morning downtime quickly became synonymous with Netflix Kids time—a designated time of relief for me, my green light for a shower, perhaps some makeup, my opportunity to go to the bathroom audience-free. Ellie loved TV time, too. As soon as we arrived home from morning errands, she would giggle with excitement and ask, "Watch show?" And I would happily oblige.

I thought, *My daughter is so smart!* And she is. She knew when TV time was coming. And she began to anticipate it earlier, and earlier, and *earlier* in the day.

One day, upon dropping Isaiah off at school, I said, "Ellie! Let's go to the grocery store and get a cookie!"

Ellie typically enjoys the grocery store well enough. We always get a free cookie, after all. So, I was surprised to hear her respond with crying and screaming, "Noooo! Go home and watch show!"

Another day, we were getting ready to head out the door *before* school, and Ellie suggested, "Stay home and watch show?"

One morning, she had just woken up. She was wiping sweet sleep from her eyes, and her first words of the day were: "Watch Elmo?"

My kids make a lot of comments and observations throughout the day. Until we started looking for the influence of screens, Jamie and I didn't really think much of these comments. We were missing the forest for the trees. We handled each comment individually, one at a time. When Ellie whined and pitched a fit for TV, we would discipline with kindness. When she had become too attached to her TV shows, we would take it away for a day, a few days, even a week—always reintroducing screens as she "earned" them back. This pattern continued until the cycle of restlessness was in full effect.

Then, there was Isaiah, our five-year-old. We noticed that his daily routine was also evolving ever so slightly and disturbingly as well. Every day, he went to school, and he rarely watched TV before school. (I was so proud of that.) In the afternoons, he would come home and have a snack. I set the bar high for best manners before granting him a little screen time. He would have to earn it, after all.

We began to notice that Isaiah was becoming increasingly obsessed with making plans for screen time. He typically came up with reasonable suggestions: "Mama, would it be OK if I watch a show after I clean up?"

"After I eat lunch and take my plate to the sink, then can I play my video game?"

"After we have snack and Ellie takes a nap and you go teach your lessons and Papa comes home, then can I play Angry Birds on his phone?"

Yes, his anticipation of screen time became more elaborate, more detailed, and often the first thing on his mind in the morning:

"Mama, after I put shoes on and go to school and then come home and have a snack and then clean up and Ellie takes her nap and if I have good manners, then can I watch a show?"

Jamie and I encouraged Isaiah to enjoy one activity at a time, not to worry about TV time so much.

Isaiah found a way around this by hinting: "Um, I was wondering, if I could do . . . something . . ."

"Like what?"

"Umm, like maybe . . . play a game?"

If I told him, "No video games," then he would clarify that he had actually meant a *board* game.

As with any child, Isaiah's manners, self-control, and tiptoeing around the issue would only last for a short time. Just as we would do with Ellie, we would lovingly discipline Isaiah when the whining started. We didn't tolerate pitching a fit. We would ban screens for a day, a few days, a week. Even in the midst of punishment, his obsession remained: "Mama, I know that I lost TV, but maybe if I have good manners, I can get them back in two days?" Of course. We always reintroduced screens, just as soon as they were "deserved."

We were feeding the beast. Fueling their addictions. We were being, we thought, good parents in disciplining the outward behavior. We even tried our best to address the heart of the matter, but it seemed a little too abstract for even our five-year-old to understand. The heart of it was the obsession. And we always, eventually, allowed them to have it again. We were, in essence, allowing our children to hold on to their idols.

—*Do you experience restlessness in your home? Are you worn out at the end of the day by your children's demands?*

—*What parenting crutches do you rely on? What are you willing to adjust when it comes to your family's daily routine?*

—How do you address issues of boredom, whining, impatience, and short attention span with your children?

—Do your children experience a cycle of restlessness? Do feel that your children obsess about screen time? In what ways?

Chapter Two

THE SCIENCE

Proven Effects of Screen Time on Children

As I watched my children's screen obsession grow, I decided to do a bit of Internet research on the specific effects of screen time on children. In general, I found that all types of professionals recommend limiting children's screen time. Statistics show connections between increased media use and problems with brain development, sleep patterns, mental health, developmental delays, decreased social interactions, decreased interest in school, and increased risk of childhood obesity. Screen-free campaigns challenge students and their parents to unplug together as a family.[2]

Despite the research, it seems that the prevailing attitude in our modern, industrialized culture essentially says, "My family is immune to the dangers of screen time because we use screens in moderation." At least, that's how I personally felt. But I was completely mistaken in assuming that screens don't affect my family very much.

One of the most eye-opening articles that I found is a brief document at screen-free.org. It's several pages long:

two pages of facts and figures, plus a multi-page list of scientific references. Here's the short version:

> The American Academy of Pediatrics [AAP], the White House Task Force on Childhood Obesity, and others discourage any screen time for children under the age of two, and less than two hours of educational programming for older children. By these recommendations, children spend too much time with screen media, since 64% of one to two-year-olds watch an average of two hours of TV a day. Preschoolers spend up to four hours a day in front of TV. Eight to 18-year-olds average more than seven hours of media use per day.
>
> Screen time negatively impacts children's sleep; it is an important risk factor in childhood obesity; it can undermine learning abilities. The more time children engage with screens, the harder it is for them to turn screens off as they become older. Excessive screen time is linked to increased psychological issues that include difficulties with peers, poor school performance, hyperactivity, emotional swings, and conduct problems.[3]

Previously, when I read about the general overuse of screens and the associated problems, I would ironically gain a prideful, false sense of security . . . as if my family's screen routine automatically became more virtuous by comparison to others' bad habits.

Some preschoolers averaging four hours of TV every day? Well, we're nowhere near watching that much!

Yet, when I read *with my mind open* to changing my own habits, I couldn't help but think of my kids—the hyperactivity, the emotional swings, the conduct issues— the restlessness! These were the main effects that my family was experiencing. Especially my five-year-old, Isaiah.

Erratic Emotional Swings in the Highly Sensitive Child

Isaiah seemed to be on roller coaster ride of emotional immaturity. He would pitch a fit and have a crying meltdown—at some point—nearly every single day. Sometimes the tantrum lasted five minutes, sometimes 45 minutes. Sometimes it happened before dinner, sometimes in the middle of the night, sometimes while playing outside. On the surface, it seemed completely random. Jamie and I reasoned: *Maybe he's tired, maybe he's hungry, maybe this is just a phase.* We dealt with his behavior one day at a time, trying lots of different approaches to help him practice more self-control.

But it *wasn't* totally random. We began to realize that when his screen time was over, sometimes 30 minutes later, sometimes several hours later, he would have a meltdown.

Here, I'd like to explain that Isaiah is highly sensitive. I determined this by taking a simple online test at www.hsperson.com and talking with his pediatrician. Highly sensitive children feel things more deeply and with more intensity. He is also firstborn, and firstborn children are prone to demonstrate acute sensitivity as well. I had already learned how to have patience when my son melted down over sand in his shoe, tags in his shirt, or sun in his eyes. Now, I was beginning to realize that Isaiah's acute sensitivity played a role in his intense anticipation of screen time. Sometimes, it seemed as if he spent so much energy *making plans* for screen time and trying to demonstrate good behavior to *earn* his screen time that he was emotionally burned out.

Similarly, his capacity for intense emotion played out as he *engaged* in screen time. His hands and forehead would sweat. His face flushed. He got tunnel vision. It took extreme effort for him to disengage, even for a moment.

I would say, "Isaiah, please pause it and wash your hands for dinner," and he wouldn't respond at all. I would repeat myself, asking him to acknowledge me by saying, "Yes ma'am,"—and as Ginger Hubbard suggests in her book, *Don't Make Me Count to Three!*—I would remind him to obey, "all the way, right away, and with a happy heart."

So, at first, I only saw screen-related behavior as an issue of teaching my child obedience, respect, and good manners. But as I considered Isaiah's acute sensitivity, it occurred to me that it was *especially* difficult for him to listen and comprehend as I spoke to him, simply because a screen was on. When the meltdown came afterwards, maybe he *was* tired, or hungry, or overstimulated. All we knew to do was to try to teach him self-control and discipline when he demonstrated disobedience and unacceptable behavior. When part of the punishment was losing screens for a few days, the meltdowns ended. The roller coaster stopped. Isaiah was able to listen and obey much more easily.

Jamie and I couldn't draw any other logical conclusion except that screen time was simply making things harder for our son to cope with his emotions. Screen time was just too much for him to handle.

Psychology of Human Attentions

Another bit of information that I'd like to share here is a talk by Akincano Marc Weber. While I do not empathize with Weber's spiritual standpoint of Buddhism, I do find his scientific research to be sound and fascinating. (In Chapter Eight, I will address how the psychology that Weber discusses is also in line with a Christian perspective.) In his talk, Weber explains some of the psychology regarding human attentions. He describes the differences between involuntary and voluntary attention:

> Many things that enable our survival don't actually make us happy . . . Most of our attention is involuntary. Involuntary attention just goes to places that are the loudest . . . It is made for us to cope with sudden dangers that appear from nowhere for which we have not prepared. That's what involuntary attention is really good at. But if nothing jumps out of the corner, then involuntary attention is rather useless. It kind of scans . . . we look for basic gratification. If involuntary attention is not coping with danger . . . then it demands to be entertained . . .
>
> Involuntary attention [is] indispensable for sudden, dangerous things . . . but in terms of happiness, involuntary attention is really a drag. It doesn't give us a good chance to actually do things that make us content, that allow the mind to become still, or that gain particularly profound insight. For that, we need *voluntary* attention . . . which is hard won . . . It's an attention that doesn't grow quickly . . . it needs to learn staying with a chosen task and deepening relationship to that chosen task . . . But you know, we *can* stay stupid and survive.[4]

In other words, our human, instinctive ability to pay attention to our environment—the very skill that helps us to survive—is the same tendency that drives us to search for endless entertainment. Our evolutionary default is to survive and look for new comforts. *Our very nature stands in the way of contentment and true rest.*

I see this concept at work in my own life on a daily basis. Our human bent towards involuntary attention is why it takes *effort* to turn off screens and why it's so *easy* to get sucked into the TV, phones, and computers. And I feel that this is why it's so important for us as parents to teach our children to develop skills of voluntary attention: to be dedicated to a task and to sustain thoughts and imaginations on a single activity for long stretches of time. So, in a sense, we must *train* our children to fight the urge to be endlessly entertained. Screens create huge obstacles in developing voluntary attention. I began to realize that removing those obstacles at home is a logical step in helping my children to mature.

Cultural Shift from 1984 to 2014

I recently turned 30 years-old. In watching my own children grow up and in researching the effects of screen time on children, I often think about my own childhood experiences with screens. When I was a kid, there were no smartphones, no tablets, no DVDs—although my siblings and I loved our Disney video cassette tapes. We did have a Gameboy and a handheld Sega, but they were mainly reserved for road trips. We watched Saturday morning cartoons and Nickelodeon after school. (I could totally dominate my little brother on Nintendo's *Super Mario Brothers III,* and, for the record, I still can.) Our family got our first home computer when I was in the third grade. I played Minesweeper and Solitaire, and I learned how to type with Mavis Beacon. Once in a blue moon, I got to play Oregon Trail in elementary school for five minutes at a time, and my first computer class in school wasn't until the sixth grade.

If you're like me, it may be initially tempting to shrug and say, "I grew up watching TV and playing video games, and I turned out fine." But today's media is not the same as it was in the 80's. According to the scientific paper, "Quicker, Faster, Darker: Changes in Hollywood Film Over 75 Years," it is plain to see that increasingly quick scene changes in media are negatively impacting human attention.[5]

Also compare the amount of time that people spend physically looking at screens versus making social contact. This aspect of the cultural media shift over the past two decades can be seen in the following chart:

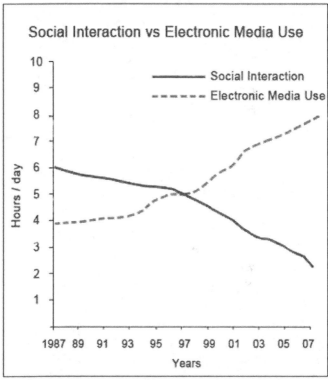

Hours per day of social interaction declines as use of electronic media increases. These trends continue beyond 2007.[6]

Research on how much time we spend making eye-to-eye contact versus eye-to-screen contact is revealing and significant. For example, a recent University of

California, Los Angeles (UCLA) study shows evidence that children's increased media use may be contributing to declining social skills: specifically, the ability to read human emotions. To quote from UCLA's website:

> "Many people are looking at the benefits of digital media in education, and not many are looking at the costs," said Patricia Greenfield, a distinguished professor of psychology in the UCLA College and senior author of the study. "Decreased sensitivity to emotional cues—losing the ability to understand the emotions of other people—is one of the costs. The displacement of in-person social interaction by screen interaction seems to be reducing social skills."[7]

Our personal experiences and science are both telling us that we are all spending more and more time in front of screens, and that our social and mental behaviors are adversely affected by this trend.

SETTING LIMITS

What some experts recommend

In 2001, the American Academy of Pediatrics [AAP] recommended that infants up to two years old should avoid screens, and that children and teens should be limited to one to two hours of screen time per day. At the time of the study, the average child consumed five hours of screen time per day.[8]

Since then, there has been an even more dramatic increase in screen use. For the first time since 2001, the AAP updated its findings in 2014:

> The average eight to ten-year-old spends nearly eight hours a day with a variety of different media, and older

children and teenagers spend up to 11 hours per day. Presence of a television set in a child's bedroom increases these figures even more, and 71% of children and teenagers report having a TV in their bedroom. Young people now spend more time with media than they do in school—it is the leading activity for children and teenagers other than sleeping.[9]

The AAP now recommends that the old two-hour limit should be applied to "entertainment" screens such as TV. Regarding all other screens, the AAP doesn't give a hard-lined answer. They encourage parents to take TVs out of their children's bedrooms. They note that "new research needs to be conducted" on the impact of media in children and adolescents. They suggest that parents "establish a family home use plan for all media," to address Internet use, cell phones, texting, and social media use.[10]

Essentially, the experts don't have the latest research that they need in order to recommend limits on all types of media. It's up to parents to decide.

Reaching My Limit with Daily Limits

In my family's experience, limiting screens to one to two hours a day is a nightmare! Since our kids are pre-schoolers, we aimed for less than one hour a day. But when I enforced the rule, the kids never felt like it was enough. It just seemed to whet their appetites for more than I was willing to allow. So, things became complicated. Isaiah and Ellie would watch TV together. One child would pick out one show, the other would pick out the next. But they each wanted more of their own show. So, Isaiah had the idea that they watch TV separately, so that he could watch his shows or play on a smartphone while Ellie napped. I was not happy with his suggestion. The heart of the matter was their screen obsession, flourishing and growing day by day. They became frustrated, and I became more frustrated.

When I let the one-hour rule slide, the restlessness and emotional meltdowns would increase in intensity and dominate the household. So, Jamie and I decided that if the cycle of restlessness was ever going to end, we had *no choice left* but to create a screen-free environment for our kids

---

—In reading about the science and psychological effects of screens, what stands out to you the most?

—What negative screen-time effects, if any, have you noticed in your household?

—What do you define as "appropriate" or "moderate" screen time in your home? Do you feel a struggle to maintain those boundaries personally and enforcing them with your children? Are your children content within the boundaries that you set?

Chapter Three

A NEW PERSPECTIVE

Giving Up Prideful Parenting

I recently read that Steve Jobs was "a low-tech parent." *New York Times* contributor Nick Bilton was surprised to hear Mr. Jobs say that his children had never even used an iPad. It turns out that many top executives of tech companies, whom you'd think would be advocates for the benefits of screen time for children, actually parent their own children with strict screen-time limitations. Here's a snippet from the *Times* article:

> How do tech moms and dads determine the proper boundary for their children? In general, it is set by age. Children under 10 seem to be most susceptible to becoming addicted, so these parents draw the line at not allowing any gadgets during the week. On weekends, there are limits of 30 minutes to two hours on iPad and smartphone use. And 10- to 14-year-olds are allowed to use computers on school nights, but only for homework.
>
> "We have a strict no screen time during the week rule for our kids," said Lesley Gold, founder and chief executive of the SutherlandGold Group, a tech media relations and analytics company. "But you have to make

allowances as they get older and need a computer for school."[11]

I was beginning to accept the fact that screens often negatively affect children—even *my* children. Along the way, it occurred to me that, technically, it would be impossible to know the true *extent* of those effects unless I removed screens altogether. I took into consideration that *everyone* in our household was frustrated with daily allowances of screen time.

A Paradigm Shift

In making the decision to get rid of the kids' screens at home, Jamie and I were challenged to change the way that we *thought*. Why *did* I think that it would be so impossible to get rid of the crutch? Why *couldn't* I imagine my kids living screen-free?

Because I was so tired! I couldn't afford to lose that 24 minutes of peace. It was too high a price, because I couldn't rely on the kids having playtime on their own when I needed them to occupy themselves.

It's a sad feeling, admitting to having such low expectations for your family. It's not as if my kids *never* played on their own. They did. Just usually not on their own initiative. I would announce, "It's time to go play!" and threaten them with, "OK, it's either playtime or naptime!" After they stalled as long as they could by asking for a snack, asking about TV time, asking, "Is Papa almost home?"—after all this, then, they would go play, for maybe 20 or 30 minutes, or 45 on a really good day. Hardly worth it when I'd spent 20 minutes making it happen!

I thought, *Eh, they're still young. They're only five and two years old. I can't expect them to play on their own for hours at a time. They'll learn when they get older. It takes time.*

And, it *does* take time. But not years. Not even months. It's a week or two. I'm serious. My kids learned how to play naturally, without me having to beg them in a matter of about 10 days. Now, instead of waking up and asking for TV shows, they wake up as a puppy, as a butterfly, as a dinosaur. They get lost in their imaginary worlds. They play together; they play separately. It's just what they're used to now.

Had I only *known* that giving up screens would pave the way for my children to play own their own initiative—for hours on end—in a matter of days, I would have given up screens in my home a *long* time ago.

Speak from the Heart with Your Children

It is not only my responsibility to enforce rules, but also to get to the heart of the issue with my children. I must take the initiative to talk with my kids about the impact that screens have in our lives. I need to be openly honest about my *own* need for discipline in using screens. I should explain that watching too much screen time is unhealthy for children *and* adults. I should be demonstrating day to day what it looks like to have good screen habits—considering others when I use my phone, using discernment in choosing what I watch, exercising good screen etiquette. So, before you jump into new rules, start discussing the risks of media use with your children now.

I remember one of the first conversations that I had with Isaiah on the subject. He was talking about a friend who "gets to watch as much TV as he wants."

Instead of immediately questioning the validity of his story, I simply said, "Wow, then I guess he must watch TV a lot. I usually get a headache if I watch too much TV.

Sometimes, I think it makes me grouchy. Did you know that watching too much TV is unhealthy?"

We talked about it for a bit. I told him that our brains need good exercise, and that's especially true for kids. I told him that one of the best ways that kids can exercise their brains is to play and imagine. He giggled at the idea of exercising his brain. And then, that was that. It didn't turn into a conversation about how he wanted to watch as much TV as he wanted, or how he just wanted to watch an episode then and there. We just had a nice talk and moved on to something else.

In starting a conversation with my kids about excess screen time, they begin to consider the risks for themselves. In explaining to children that too much screen time is unhealthy, I use the analogy of chocolate cake. "I love to eat chocolate cake. But I would feel sick if I eat too much of it, or even if I eat it for breakfast." Even little kids can understand this much, and that's a great start.

Spinning Plates

Parenting is complicated. Even the most basic responsibilities that come with having kids adds up fast: providing healthy meals, putting clothes on their backs, and finding shoes to fit their growing feet. Then there's keeping up with the laundry, the dishes, the vacuuming, paying the bills, going to work, ensuring we are getting enough exercise, *and* monitoring screen time.

I am continually looking for ways to make it easier to keep all of my plates spinning. I love finding a new, easy recipe. I love a good consignment sale. I take pride in doing housework, even though I fall behind. (Who doesn't fall behind?) I appreciate learning a practical step to tighten up the family budget. I get excited about new ideas for teaching music classes. I'm enjoying my new yoga routine. So, what could possibly make the daily chore of *monitoring* screen time easier than *simply removing* screens from the house?

Removing screens from my home makes the plate of responsibility much easier for me to spin; however, it does not eliminate the plate altogether. Screens are accessible almost everywhere, which means that my responsibility as a parent to *monitor* my children's screen time remains. I still have to make sure that my children's screen time is appropriate in its content and the amount of time they're using it, even if they are not using screens at home.

Having "The Talk" About Digital Safety

As our children become adolescents, we, the parents, must teach them about adult realities, *well before* it's time for them to experience those things—for example, earning a living, driving, managing money, consuming alcohol, becoming sexually active. We have to explain and model the responsibilities: how to balance the risks and the joys of adult life. We need to have lots of little *talks* with our kids . . . about adult things, before they become adults.

While my children are still young, I have the opportunity to teach them about digital safety—*before* it becomes something that they deal with on a daily basis. Open up lines of communication with your child to discuss the responsibilities, risks, and joys of screen time. There are many resources available on how to educate your child about online safety. Two such resources that I have found particularly helpful are NetSmartz and the Family Online Safety Institute. There are free, printable activities like flashcards and family contracts to help start those important conversations with your child.

Leticia Barr, writer of TechSavvyMama.com has laid

out some very helpful guidelines regarding when and how to address screen safety with your children: [12]

- **Toddlers & preschoolers:** Even though children this young should not be dealing with screens, they are aware of them. Explain to young children the cake analogy—that too much of a good thing can be unhealthy. Explain that adults use screens to do work. Model good screen etiquette for your child. Be aware that if your young child is using apps, that she may be tempted to click on ads and make purchases.

- **K-2nd graders:** A child in this age group may be asked to use the internet for homework. If this is the case, then be sure to come alongside them and put parental controls in place. Explain to your child that some websites are unsafe; empower him to tell you if he ever sees something suspicious, mean, or scary online. Class discussion boards may also be a part of his homework, so talk to your child about the importance of being nice online. This will lay the groundwork for discussing cyberbullying when he is older. Discuss marketing tactics that tempt kids to click on things online, to buy apps, etc. Children need to learn that not all adults have their best interest at heart.

- **Tweens (8-12 year olds):** Many tweens spend time online perusing YouTube videos and playing games online. While your child may not be doing these activities at home, he may be exposed to it elsewhere. Cox and the National Center for Missing & Exploited Children have found that 42% of 10- to 13-year olds have received messages from people they've never met. [13] Discuss things like cyberbullying, and reinforce that your child can always come to you to discuss screen activity. Talk about how to use screens well, that screens can be helpful in completing a task; however, screens can be time-wasters when they are not used wisely.

- **Teenagers:** Texting, driving, and Facebook, oh my. Did I mention that it's best to start early and often with these little talks? Hopefully, healthy lines of communication are available with your teenager so that you can further discuss and establish ground rules and trust. Teenagers should be especially careful to avoid online drama. Discuss what it is to have a digital reputation; remind them to always think before posting something online. Emphasize that using social media is not the same as being social.

As you can see, simply because a child doesn't use screens at home on a daily basis, he still must learn about online safety. It is a hugely important topic, and we should be sure to discuss it as much as possible with our children, long before they have to deal with it.

—*Do you rely on screen time as a parenting crutch? How often?*

—*Does it seem too extreme to be screen-free at home? Why or why not?*

—If you knew for certain that your children would learn to play happily for longer than their routine screen time, would you be willing to give up screens at home?

—What are some ways that you can start discussing online safety with your child? Take time to look at websites such as netsmartz.org and familyonlinesafetyinstitute.org.

Chapter Four

THE NEW NORMAL

Screen-Free at Home Until Age 12

My recommendation for kids' screen-time has two parts:
(1) screen-free at home and (2) until age 12.

Screen-Free at Home

I don't feel the need to shield my children from all
screens everywhere. Our parents want to take Isaiah to a
movie? Great. Ellie watches kids' TV shows at the gym
childcare? No problem. Those situations happen
regularly, sprinkled into their schedules, outside of our
home.

Regarding inside the home, well, it's our home. We
can choose not to make screens an option for our
children in our house until they are 12 or whenever we
decide. The scientifically proven effects of screen
exposure, coupled with my family's personal experiences,
have convinced me that providing my children a screen-
free home is in our best interest.

Let's go back to the journalist, Nick Bilton, who
interviewed Steve Jobs and other technologists. Bilton

notes that most tech leaders practice limiting screens in their own parenting, while "others said that outright bans could backfire and create a digital monster." For example:

> Dick Costolo, chief executive of Twitter, told me he and his wife approved of unlimited gadget use as long as their two teenage children were in the living room. They believe that too many time limits could have adverse effects on their children.
>
> "When I was at the University of Michigan, there was this guy who lived in the dorm next to me and he had cases and cases of Coca-Cola and other sodas in his room," Mr. Costolo said. "I later found out that it was because his parents had never let him have soda when he was growing up. If you don't let your kids have some exposure to this stuff, what problems does it cause later?" [14]

I understand Costolo's point that a complete ban could backfire, which is the reason that I intentionally do not shield my children's eyes from every screen everywhere. Even when I take the occasional picture of the kids on my phone at home (which is much less often now than what it used to be!), I ask them if they want to see it afterwards.

However, I see a complete ban on screens with no exceptions at one end of the extreme, and unlimited screen time on the other end. My version of being screen-free is not *completely* screen-free. In practice, it's kind of like a diet that you intentionally cheat on from time to time. For example, screens are a daily reality for adults. Jamie and I have smartphones; we send emails and texts on a daily basis; I use the computer to pay bills; and, while I much prefer working with pen and paper, I am ultimately using a computer to write this book. Yet, Jamie and I avoid using these things around the kids as much as possible, although it is unavoidable at times. The kids understand that we are using screens to complete necessary tasks, not to endlessly entertain ourselves. The kids themselves are given no screen time opportunities at all at home, saved for *very few* exceptions.

Until Age 12

Children have so much to learn. There are so many habits to cultivate and skills to grasp: language, education, social etiquette, healthy eating habits, good sleep patterns. These things are as much a responsibility for the child to learn as they are for the parents to teach. Then, adolescence will kick in, and our children will start becoming adults.

Adults today grew up with limited exposure to less sophisticated screen technology; however, screens—in greater quantity and variety—are an inevitable part of our world now. Internet use, emails, and texting are a daily reality for adults. It's a significant responsibility to navigate the digital world in a healthy way, and a child should not be burdened with such a task. Daily screen use is simply not a necessary part of a child's daily life. So, only when my children are ready and of an appropriate age, about twelve years old, then I will do as the AAP recommends and adjust my family media use plan, gradually allowing screen time for my kids, little by little, as they get older.

Exceptions to the Rule

There are *always* exceptions to rules. If you don't plan on them, they will happen more often than you would like. Here's what happened the first time that we made an exception.

It was steamy, rainy, summer day, about 1:00 in the afternoon. We were driving home from the library. In the backseat, Ellie was looking at a book about ballet. Isaiah glanced up from his *Diary of a Wimpy Kid* and said, "Ballet is just *not* cool."

I said, "What?! Ballet is *really* cool! It is *the* most difficult type of dance to learn. Girls *and* boys take ballet. The boys who do ballet are very strong—they even pick up other dancers off of the floor!"

He scrunched up his face. He wasn't buying it.

I hesitated. There are several issues at play here: First, Isaiah is really into dance. He loves it. He dances at home all the time, and he had enjoyed taking dance class the previous year. Second, I had recently watched a documentary, *First Position*, about kids from all over the world who go to New York to compete for scholarships to ballet academies and contracts for prestigious dance companies. It is an amazing film, and I couldn't help but think that Isaiah *and* Ellie would love watching it. Third, up to that day, Isaiah and Ellie had been screen-free at home for about two months. Those two months had been so transformative, and I didn't want to ruin it by tempting them with a screen at home. Wouldn't I be running the risk of starting the cycle of restlessness all over again?

But I took a chance—that movie is inspirational and educational. Dance is *movement*. It needs to be experienced visually. We could read about it and talk about it, but it wouldn't be the same as *watching* it.

So, I started telling the kids all about the documentary as we drove home. Isaiah was in disbelief that boys do ballet. As we pulled in the driveway, I asked the kids, "Would you like to watch it altogether?"

Ellie said, "Ballerina!"

Isaiah said, "Um, well, sure, I guess so."

So, we watched it. I watched for red flags, but I didn't notice any. Isaiah's hands and face didn't become sweaty. Ellie giggled and commented throughout: "Like Ellie! Ballerina!" I was able to talk *with* them while we watched. We ate popcorn, and about 45 minutes in, the kids wanted to take a break from watching. They actually *asked* if I would pause it. It blew my mind. We finished the second half of the movie and discussed how cool it was. When the movie was over, I braced myself for a possible emotional meltdown or whining or restlessness. But they handled it just fine.

Decide How Often

We make an exception for family screen time at home once every couple of months. It may sound ridiculous, but it's worked out really well for us.

Many low-tech parents allow screens on the weekends, and if you have older children, that may work for you. The key is to decide ahead of time instead of allowing more than you plan.

For our family, screens on the weekends is too much. Even just once a week or more fuels the restlessness. Once every few weeks is flirting with danger, too. So, for us, once every couple of months it is. I try to choose an educational program or a movie night just for fun. We make a point to have everyone in the family participate together.

Going back to the chocolate cake analogy: Sometimes, it helps me to think of screen time as *birthday* cake. We host friends or family members' birthdays *in our home* once in a blue moon. We count by the months and years, not by the day. Birthday parties are a happy occasion, something to look forward to, and something to experience together as a family. I think that screen time for a child, in his or her home, should be a similar experience.

Decide For What Reasons

In my example with *First Position*, I felt that I had stumbled upon a unique opportunity to share something educational and exciting with my children. The movie sparked family conversation; it inspired the kids to dance, and it renewed their enthusiasm for dance class each week. A *screen* helped create those opportunities, and I celebrate that!

So, decide ahead of time *why* you would allow an exception to your rule. Is it enough of a reason that the kids just really want to and have been complaining for a long time? Consider what positive or negative consequences may come about down the line from allowing screen time in your home.

Discern What is Truly Educational

"Have you heard about this new app for kids? It is so educational!"

"My preschooler just loves PBS.org!"

"My kids love to watch Sesame Street, and they learn so much from it."

I hear comments like this often. Before we pulled the plug, I used to say these things myself. It felt good to justify my kids' daily screen time by touting educational benefits. This mindset is deeply ingrained in our culture. In fact, it is common for even very young children to be required to use screens for homework. If this is the case for your child, then monitor those situations carefully. If children are rewarded at school by being allowed to bring their own screens into the classroom, then start a conversation with your child—and perhaps with the school administration.

While many children's screen activities are marketed as "educational," we as parents should be wary of those labels. The AAP asserts that young children learn more efficiently and effectively from non-screen sources.[15] Choose a real book instead of an app; a tactile game instead of a virtual game.

Once again going back to the *First Position* example, I stand by my decision that watching it as a family was a healthy exception to our rule. The movie is truly educational because it portrays true and powerful stories of young people working diligently to achieve their goals. Ironically, the movie is not specifically marketed to children. It is simply a family-friendly documentary.

Still, it would have been ideal for the kids to have the opportunity to experience a live ballet. But, I considered their ages, the timeliness of the conversation, and overall convenience, and I chose the next-best thing. Let's acknowledge that, compared to tangible, real experiences, screens merely provide a *second*-best opportunity for education.

It's "Brain-Dead Easy"

I often hear parents—half bewildered, half bragging—tell stories about how quickly their toddler learned how to use screens. "It was as if she automatically knew what to do! It's amazing. I just think it's great for kids to learn how to use this stuff as early as possible."

Yes, screen technology *is* amazingly intuitive. Tech companies want to make their products as user-friendly as possible. But, no, that shouldn't necessarily be a reason to promote screen time for young children. Alan Eagle, a Google executive communications staffer and father of two, says: Learning how to use screens is "super-easy . . . brain-dead easy . . . There's no reason why kids can't figure it out when they get older."[16]

Parents may fear that their child may be left behind or left out if she is not exposed to screens early on; however, there is no evidence that a screen-free child will be unable to "catch up" to her tech-savvy peers. I also wonder: Just how "tech-savvy" can a toddler be? A toddler may be able to navigate her way around an app, but she is merely demonstrating intuitive, knee-jerk, "brain-dead" abilities. A screen-free child, on the other hand, is given distinct educational opportunities to *play*, which is "essential to cognitive, physical, social, and emotional development."[17] A screen-free child can also uniquely learn about digital safety *before* having to deal with screens. In other words, avoid screens in order to give your child the best opportunities to develop healthily and to learn how to use screens *well* for when the time is right.

Sharing Your Decision

Sometimes, people ask me how my extended family reacted to our decision to go screen-free. The simple answer is that everyone has been very supportive. When we made the decision to go screen-free at home, Jamie and I never exactly declared it to anyone. We didn't exactly know how things would turn out ourselves. But, a couple of weeks in, we became increasingly amazed by our children's improving behavior, so we began sharing our experience with friends and family.

In fact, I haven't encountered very much negative feedback whatsoever. That may miraculously be because each and every person completely agrees with us. However, I think that one simple explanation may be that it hardly affects anyone else directly.

Since the basic premise is to be screen-free *at home*,

no one outside of our home necessarily *realized* that we had decided to go screen-free. It really only directly affects people who are in our home. Also, there are so many exceptions to our decision: (1) it only strictly applies until they turn 12; (2) we are not turning a blind eye to all of the screens around us; (3) we don't demonize screens or act as if screens are completely absent from our house, and (4) we even make exceptions to enjoy screens at home together. In other words, I do not feel that we are taking an extreme position.

Still, before we ventured into this screen-free territory, when I hadn't given much thought to the effects of screen time, I was skeptical and cynical when I heard of families who drastically cut back their screen time. And, considering how much I relied on screen time every day with the kids, I was opposed to trying it myself. So, understand that others may argue with your decision and respond with skepticism. But, the way I see it now, skepticism is a great place to be, because *that skeptic was me* less than one year ago. In other words, this book is written *for* skeptics *by* a skeptic.

Your family and friends may not be as understanding as mine were if you decide to go screen-free. So, if you are confronted with negative responses, my advice is, don't worry about it. Sympathize with their skepticism, and share confidently anyway. People rarely change their perspectives overnight. In fact, the first thing that people may notice is your child's drastically improved behavior— and who could argue against that?

For example, when we happened to mention to our parents that the kids had been screen-free at home for some time and that we saw an increased attention span, our parents were happy for us and said, "That's great." Soon after, they kept the kids for a Saturday afternoon at their house. When we picked up the kids at the end of the day, our parents exclaimed, "We had such a great time! The kids played outside at the sand table for an hour and a half! We've never seen them so content to play one thing for so long! We know that you mentioned that their attention span has gotten better, but we're just blown away."

No matter what response you may get, remember that you're the parent, and you have every right to decide what is best for your family.

—Does screen-free at home until 12 with a few exceptions sound reasonable to you? What adjustments would you make to the rule?

—How often and for what reasons would you make an exception and allow screen time in your home?

—What educational opportunities would your children have more time for if they did not have access to screens at home?

—Do you anticipate that extended family or friends may respond negatively to your decision to cut back on screen time?

Chapter Five

THE EXPECTATIONS

So, we committed to providing a screen-free home for our children. What came next was an uncomfortable transition period of about 10 days. Transitioning children to a screen-free home *will* produce wonderful changes, and it will also be quite an adjustment for everyone in the family. For me, the inconveniences became tolerable, even enjoyable, especially as I began to see wonderful changes surfacing in the kids' behavior. In the days, weeks, and months to follow, the benefits that the entire family enjoyed turned out to be more dramatic than we ever expected.

Face Your Fears

First, let's tackle the fears may be holding you back from committing to going screen-free in your home. Here are some negative expectations that I had and that I often hear others wonder about.

"What will I *do*?"
People sometimes say to me: "That's great that you've cut out screen time at home, but I don't understand.

What do you *do*? How do you fill the time? How do you get a break?" I completely understand.

There are so many things that, as a parent, you *have* to plan out for your child. You have to *tell them* that it's time to get dressed, eat breakfast, get shoes on, go to school, go to activities, wash hands, go to the bathroom, eat dinner, wash up, put on PJ's, brush teeth, go to bed. Those are non-negotiable, scheduled activities where your child learns to listen and obey as you explain what "it's time for."

Then, there are the in-between times when *you* need to get something done: pack lunches, clean up, fix dinner, take a shower, do laundry, pay bills, make phone calls, and Lord-willing, maybe even take a break. During these times, I couldn't rely on the kids to entertain themselves for very long, so I would announce "It's screen time!" in hopes of a set amount of time to get something accomplished.

I was planning everything, all of the time, and making no differentiation between the non-negotiables of the day and when the kids might otherwise have free time. For my own convenience, I would decide *for* them how they should spend their free time: usually with a screen, and sometimes by sending them upstairs to play by themselves—*if* I felt that I would have the patience to deal with the aftermath of a mess and whining. So, as a rule of thumb, if I wanted a shower, it was time for a kids' TV show.

So, the question of, "What will I *do?*" arises out of the assumption that you will have to *continue* to plan out every activity for your child. The reality is that you should start differentiating between when it's time to tell your kids what to do and when they should have some freedom to decide how to spend their time. As Dr. Aric Sigman says, "One of the greatest gifts that we can offer our children is the gift of boredom."[18] That is when your kids will truly *learn how to play on their own*.

Now, when I need to take a shower and the kids are around, I don't assume that there will be mass chaos if I don't flip on the TV. Turning on a screen never guaranteed peace and quiet anyway. No, now I just go take a shower. In passing, I let them know where I'll be, and usually they are doing their own thing. They are mature enough to safely play in the house unsupervised. If they need me, they know where to find me.

"It will take so much energy—and I am *already* exhausted."

Yes. Making the transition *does* take a lot of effort, and if you're like me, you feel like you have little or no energy to spare. But the extra effort and energy is only needed during that short, ten-day-ish transition time. After that, your investment of a little effort will greatly pay off in gaining time to relax in your own home. Instead of feeling tired for no good reason with no end in sight, you will know that your tiredness in the time of transition is no longer in vain!

For me, the first few days of avoiding kid screen time was rough. I was a real wimp about it. As soon as Jamie and I put the kids to bed, we would binge-watch episodes of *The Office* and eat chocolate on the couch for hours. Our inside joke was that the *less* TV the kids watched, the *more* TV we needed to watch in order to cope with the exhaustion. We laughed to keep from crying. But that feeling only lasted a short while. On the difficult transition days, keep that ten-day time frame in mind.

Not only will your children transition out of their screen habits, but also, you will transition away from a feeling of needing to crash at the end of every day to experiencing what it means to *rest well*. You will also find pockets of rest throughout the day, and you will have time to breathe while the kids learn how to play contentedly for longer and longer stretches of time.

"Won't my child feel like he is missing out?"

At first, he may feel like he is missing out, but in the long run, he is not going to feel deprived. A *little* screen time goes a *long* way, and it doesn't need to be at home.

Isaiah went with his grandparents to see the movie *Frozen* when it came out in theaters. He loved it. He still remembers all of the characters, all of the songs. It doesn't take much, because reminders are everywhere! *Frozen* themed toys, books, fruit snacks, pajama sets, songs playing in public places, you name it. Isaiah is *in the know*, along with all of his peers, because he had *one* experience with it. I am not obligated to buy the DVD so that he can relive it 1,000 more times.

A little screen time away from home is enough for toddlers, too. While we were on family vacation this summer, we let the kids watch 20 minutes of TV at the hotel. They saw *part of one episode* of Doc McStuffins, and it is now Ellie's favorite thing. When we're out and about, she tracks down Doc McStuffins paraphernalia like a hawk.

So, for example, while the three of us are wandering around Target, it is not even a temptation to buy a $20 DVD. On the other hand, I might decide to indulge them with the $3 box of character fruit snacks or the $2 coloring books or the $1 sticker sets. Win-win, right? Well, as I will discuss this later in Chapter Seven, I am not obligated to buy all of the inexpensive paraphernalia, either.

"I just don't know. Will it be worth it? I can just picture the temper tantrums now!"

Yes, yes, and yes. It's true that you *don't* know, simply because you haven't yet experienced it for yourself. You *won't* know for sure until you give it a try. Also, because I am a wimpy mama who has tried it and reached the other side, I want to reassure you that yes, it *will* be worth it. And yes, there will probably be some temper tantrums, and I don't handle temper tantrums well. Sometimes, I even throw in my own dramatic reaction. (I wonder where they learn that behavior?) Sometimes things get a little worse before they get better, and that's OK. As much as I used to feel uncomfortable dealing with my kids' tantrums, I actually felt secure in the midst of their fits once we had made the decision to go screen-free. In other words, my kids' overblown reactions affirmed to me that we had made the right decision.

One of the first times that I had to say no when our screen-free journey began, I simply told Ellie, "No Elmo right now, honey." She proceeded to scream, slobber, and roll around on the kitchen floor in a fit of despair.

I remember it well. I was surprised at how calm I felt. I thought, *Yeahhh, this is a pretty good indication that she has a problem. She needs help. She's just a baby.* So, I told her, "I love you," I washed some dishes, and I gave her a big hug when she was finished pitching her fit. Of course, I explained that she shouldn't act like that, but I felt responsible for allowing her TV addiction to form in the first place. I reassured her again that I loved her, and it felt good knowing that I was helping her in the best way that I knew how, instead of selfishly giving in to her demands for screen time for the sake of my own convenience.

"I don't think that I have the patience."

Impatience is one of the main reasons that I refer to myself as a wimpy mama. I am anxious, impatient, and often grouchy. So, if I can do it, anyone can. On a note of tough love, let me share a quote from the diet professionals at Whole 30:

> Don't you dare tell us this is hard. Beating cancer is hard. Birthing a baby is hard. Losing a parent is hard. Drinking your coffee black. Is. Not. Hard. [19]

Indeed, the inconveniences of banning screens from your children is a first-world problem, friends. You can do it!

Changes to Look Forward To

Ultimately, a screen-free home *lifts a burden* for children *and* parents. When children do not have the option to use screens at home, there is no more day in, day out, power struggle. The whining for it, the zoning out when you need them to pay attention, the obsession throughout the day—the restlessness—fades away. Here are a few of the changes that we experienced in our home.

Expectations Exceeded: Kids Play for Hours

After about 10 days of keeping a screen-free home, I noticed the kids were engaging in unprompted playtime for longer periods of time. Soon, they were spending hours contentedly imagining, exploring, and playing, where they previously played for only 20, 30, or maybe 45 minutes before becoming restless. (Of course, your results may vary depending on your child's current dependency on screens, her age, her personality, and other factors.)

As we gave up screens at home, I couldn't *wait* for the restlessness to subside. Yet, when instances of restful, contented play manifested, I felt so blown away.

After a few weeks of being screen-free, I was reading in the living room while the kids were playing upstairs. I heard Isaiah coming downstairs asking, "Mama, could we play Lego Star Wars?"

I hesitated. Lego Star Wars is a video game that he played at home before I took away screens. Incidentally, it's a cool game. I said, "Well, it's not really time for playing Wii right now."

Then I looked at him. He was holding a Luke Skywalker Lego minifigure and a ship that he had built. He looked confused. "Oh. Well, we *could* play it on the screen, but real life is more fun."

It took me a second to realize that he was not testing the water to see if I would let him play a video game. He was *inviting me to play Lego*. Given the choice between video game or reality, he preferred to act as characters in our own make-believe game.

"Isaiah, that's a great idea. I would love to play. May I be Yoda?"

Child Becomes Restful and Initiates Play

As mentioned in Chapter Three, children rest better when they are not overstimulated. Dr. Sigman elaborates on "the gift of boredom" by explaining that "by giving [children] an enforced absence of stimulation, there are measurable improvements in a variety of things, from creativity to calmness."[20]

So, one of the main benefits of screen-free living is watching your child grow in her freedom to initiate her own play. When you create a screen-free environment for your child to thrive, there be an inevitable and wonderful shift in your child's demeanor again.

Eventually, she will be more calm, more content, less needy, less whiny. Instead of complaining about having nothing to do, she will announce, "I'm going upstairs to play!" She will naturally develop a habit of initiating playtime. Again, this may take some time depending on a child's age and personality.

Imaginations Bloom

I used to feel the need to "help" the kids play pretend. I thought, *Maybe if I get them started playing something fun, they will continue on their own.* It usually took them a while to get into it, and the magic fizzled quickly.

Now that we have been screen-free for some time, the first thing that Isaiah and Ellie do each morning is announce that they are cats, butterflies, Pokémon characters, or dinosaurs . . . and by the time we are downstairs eating breakfast, they have changed to puppies, penguins, or rabbits. I can barely keep up with their rich, imaginative play. They have an *eagerness* to pretend. They come up with ideas more quickly than I could have ever conjured up on my own.

More Content, Less Fidgety

Car rides and restaurant experiences used to really stress me out. The kids would fidget and whine about how long it was taking, so I felt obligated to bring an arsenal of distractions to keep them occupied. But being screen-free has truly helped their level of contentment and enjoyment. They have learned to be content with a single book in the car and to enjoy the experience of eating at a restaurant, seated the entire time. Perhaps a younger, more energetic child may not exhibit these exact same abilities; however, it is realistic to expect any child to be more content overall.

Improved Mood and Sleep Patterns

In removing screens, you enable your child to rest in so many ways. Isaiah sleeps much more soundly than he ever has, now that we are screen-free. Ellie used to typically wake up grouchy, crying, asking when she could watch her TV show. Now, she typically wakes up happy and content to play in her bed until I get her out.

— *How long do you think that it would take your family to adjust to a screen-free routine?*

— *What positive changes do you think that you would see in your own children? In you and your partner?*

— *How difficult do you think that it would be to make the transition? What would be the hardest part?*

Chapter Six

THE TRANSITION

To adjust to this new way of life, you should not merely replace screens with alternate activities for your children. We need to give our children ample opportunity to rest and to give *voluntary attention* to their play.

You have lots of tools to stake out this new territory. There are practical steps that you can daily to get into that new rhythm of life. So, here's my bag of tricks: new habits to adopt, phrases to use, ideas to try—so that you will feel prepared for the bumps along the way.

Put Down Your Phone and Keep the TV Off.

I was chatting with a friend about my family's screen-free experiences, and she seemed confused. She asked, "How do you get your *husband* to keep the TV off all day?"

You and your partner must commit together to improve your own screen etiquette. It is probably safe to assume that one partner is a little more addicted to screens than the other. For example, in our marriage, I'm the bigger addict. Jamie can take it or leave it, but there are times when I count down the *minutes* until the kids' bedtime, simply because it's the ideal opportunity to sneak off and watch *Mad Men*. So, keep your own screens off until your kids are in bed, *even if* your favorite show or smartphone game happens to be kid-friendly.

Only use your phone around the kids when it's absolutely necessary. Explain what you're doing ahead of time. Make eye contact with your kids and apologize, as you would with any other person: "I'm sorry, I need to take this call right now," or, "Please excuse me for five minutes while I send this important work email." When you're done, give your kids your full attention once again. Now, when the kids see me on the phone, they know, "Mama's working, and I should not interrupt her, but she will answer my question when she is done."

Cheerfully Say, "It's not time for screens right now."

Say it over, and over, and over. Say it with love. Realize that, as much as you will tell them *no*, the kids will continue to ask for screens. After all, it was a daily part of their life. Try not to get frustrated simply because they keep asking.

Change the Way You Talk About Screens.

In observing my personal attitude towards screens, I noticed that I talked with my kids about screens as if screens were *the ultimate reward*, a wonderful *privilege* that yes, may very well be taken away if they misbehaved. "Losing games," as we referred to it, was absolutely the *most* dreaded punishment.

"You lost TV for tomorrow." "No iPhone games for three days." "No computer time for a week." Give up these crutches.

Taking away screens should not be used as a form of punishment. For a child, being screen-free should be a normal and wonderful aspect of their everyday life. There is no need to make a big deal about it, to manipulate their feelings, or to gain an edge of power by dangling the possibility of losing or gaining screen time over their heads.

As I mentioned earlier, talking about the unhealthy side-effects of screens with your children is important. However, it may be best to wait until they have been screen-free for a while before preaching it and going into the birthday cake analogy. Keep it as positive as possible in the beginning. Avoid demonizing their desires.

Acknowledge, Be Direct, Redirect.

Depending on how heavily your children currently use screens, they will understandably be upset when they're gone. Your children's emotional reactions should be handled with empathy, patience, firmness, and caring. They will be confused and frustrated. To help sympathize, make sure to acknowledge their feelings, to be direct in telling them that screens are not an option, and to help redirect their attention to another activity.

Example: Toddlers

It had been about two months since we'd gone screen-free, and I was working at our home computer. Ellie came up and asked, "Watch Daniel Tiger?" (Sometimes, when Ellie asks for screen time, all I do is acknowledge her enthusiasm for screens, and the issue resolves itself. Other times, I go on to suggest another activity.)

I smiled at her and said, "Oh, I love Daniel Tiger!"

Ellie paused and repeated, "Watch Daniel Tiger?"

I say, "No, Mama's working right now, so we're not going to watch Daniel Tiger. But I could take a break. Hey, do you want to *play* Daniel Tiger with me? I'll be Katerina Kitty Cat!" I enthusiastically meow.

Redirecting to a new activity doesn't usually take much effort with toddlers. You may have to step away from your own activity for a bit, and your toddler may not be completely happy with your idea at first, but make it a habit to respond this way. A little quality time is most likely just what your child needs.

Ellie blinked and replied with a smile, "No, *I* be Katerina."

Example: Ages 5 and Older
Simple diversions and a bit of attention can also help older children feel that they are not missing out on screen time at home.

Recently, Isaiah was going on and on about how much he wanted to play the aforementioned Lego Star Wars video game. He wasn't really whining, but he was excited and hopeful that I would let him play it.

I told him, "Yes, I like that game, too, but it's not time for screens right now. Hey, I wonder if we could find a book at the library about Lego Star Wars."

He didn't seem interested, but when he saw that I was willing to take him to the library then and there, he perked up. A spontaneous change of scenery goes a long way. It was worth it to see his excitement when we found a book that he liked.

Sometimes Say, "Let's Talk About TV Later."

Sometimes, we simply can't drop everything to take a library trip. Sometimes, Isaiah continues talking about screens, plans for screens, asking questions about screens, and pushing the whole screen subject too much, so that I finally have to say, "Isaiah, honey, I just don't want to talk about screens right now. Please let's talk about them later."

This type of comment shifts the conversation from a simple back-and-forth to an issue of obedience. I am in charge, and I say it's time to change the subject. Use this approach sparingly as to not create a habit of shutting down conversations about screens. Conversation itself is a good thing, but make sure to stand your ground when it becomes whining. Obsession is evidence of addiction. More important than diverting your child's attention, help him resist his fixation with screens.

One Week Can Make a Difference

Keep in mind that this time of transition is temporary. You won't need to distract or redirect forever. The goal is to teach children to stop relying on screens at home. They will get used to it and stop asking after a time. As I mentioned, even after about two months of being screen-free, seeing the computer was still a trigger for Ellie to ask for screen time. However, after *several* months of being screen-free, seeing me work at the computer was no longer a trigger for her. After several months, the kids haven't asked for screen time at all.

Maybe you're not ready to dive in and never look back the way that I did, and that's fine. Start small—with just one week. It's better to start somewhere than not give it a shot at all! One week should be long enough to see some positive behavior changes to encourage you, but remember that it took my kids slightly longer (about 10 days) to settle into their new screen-free routine.

Because my experience is limited to my own two young children, I want to share some accounts of other families' screen-free experiences. Perhaps your children are much older than mine, or maybe you have child younger than two years. One of my favorite resources is screenfree.org, where families all over the world are challenged to unplug together for just one week. Metroparent.com followed a few of those families and reported their stories. Read about the Martin family's experience:

The Martin Family of Northville, Michigan—Bruce, father; Amy, mother; Claire, daughter age 10; Alexander, son age 9. Claire's screen time has been limited, but she recently got an iPad and has become hooked on Instagram. Amy worries it may affect her daughter's grades. Alexander loves his Xbox and joins his cousins in multiplayer games, communicating with them through headphones as they play. The kids also have a tablet. The Martins recently installed a second TV in their home and watch shows together a couple times a week. Amy enjoys Facebook and entering online contests—and takes her smartphone with her everywhere. Bruce, who owns an insurance agency, stays plugged in at all times for his customers.

Biggest challenge—From Day One, the challenge was easier than expected. The Martins read, played the Othello board game and baked together. Family dinner time stretched out longer and they chatted more. Bruce taught Alex to play chess instead of bonding over their usual TV shows. The kids played in the snow, constructed a fort and had friends over to play.

Looking back—When the kids knew video games weren't an option they didn't ask a single time, finding other things to do. The downside? "My house was trashed," Amy says. "I was stepping on Legos for a week." Overall, Amy says she felt more in the moment because she wasn't compelled to constantly check her email. "I noticed I am not 'needed' as much as electronics make me feel like I am," Amy says. "You can give people your full energy." Amy closed her computer and put it away in a drawer, so she wasn't tempted to check emails. She left her smartphone at home while doing errands. Bruce turned off his phone in the evening and realized much of his work could wait. The Martins discovered they can enjoy family time in other ways.

Going forward—The Martins had a family meeting about how to use the knowledge gained during the challenge. Bruce wants to keep screen-free dinners, and Amy vows to limit her own online engagement. "I am going to continue to work on being present with my family without distractions," Amy says. They hope their children will make better decisions on their own when it comes to using media. "You can always add more technology to your family," Amy says. "It's harder to take away."[21]

The popular blog, *Simplicity Parenting*, also features stories of families who participate in the Screen-Free Week challenge. For example, Lindsey Brady, founder of Seedlings Nursery School, writes about the dramatic change that she saw in her toddler's behavior.

It's 11:30 AM . . . you have an hour in which to feed your two-year-old son and *attempt* to get him to take a nap. You plop something down in front of him while you go about cleaning up from the morning's events; checking and replying to email; preparing and eating your own lunch and constantly reminding him that he better eat his lunch (which he is currently ignoring) so that he can go take a nap. With about 30 minutes to spare, you declare that it's time for a nap and take your little one upstairs completely wired from the morning activities and then get frustrated when he can't wind down and fall asleep in the 20 minutes you have left to accomplish the task. Eventually, you give up and finish preparations for the afternoon which is bound to be extremely difficult with an overtired, under-fed toddler on your hands.

Fast forward a week; same scenario; same two-year old . . . On this day, you give your child two choices for lunch: he can have a sandwich or some hummus. He chooses the latter and you oblige. You tell him that after lunch he can either choose to take a nap in his bed, or have quiet time upstairs in his room. He chooses quiet time and asks if you'll join him upstairs for a few minutes. You agree. He finishes eating, helps put his food away and starts upstairs on his own. After a story, a few minutes of dress-up and some marbles down the homemade paper towel tube marble track, you tell him that you have some work to do, but he can choose to have more quiet time in his room or take a nap in his bed. He asks you to stay, but after a gentle reminder that after lunch we have quiet time, he settles into the rocking chair with a book. When the hour is up, he happily rejoins you in your daily work and remains agreeable for the remainder of the day.

What happened here, you ask? Screen-Free Week, that's what! Yes, I'll admit it; that was me up there in that opening paragraph, completely unaware (or perhaps blissfully ignorant) that my personal computer usage was causing my child's unappealing behaviors.[22]

Depending on the ages of your children and what your family's routine looks like, maybe you can relate to one of these stories. Picture how your family might benefit and grow together from one week without screens.

If it is difficult to decide when to start an entire week of no screens, then start with one "screen-free" night per week. Think of fun activities that you could do together: Call it "Family game night" or "Reading night" as a first step.

Many families struggle to balance screen time during the summer or school holidays, when children may be spending hours at a time in front of screens. Set a technology-free zones in the house and specific screen-free times during holidays or weekends. Maybe you binge on screens in the evenings after work. Challenge yourself to condense your own personal screen time to 1-2 hours. As my dear friend Kate says, "Setting a boundary and a time frame at the beginning helps me to stay focused on responding to emails or catching up on social media."

Whether you choose to go all in or just start small, talk with your partner, make a commitment, and see where it takes you.

—*Do you feel a little addicted to screens? Is your partner often distracted by screens? Gently encourage one another to improve your screen etiquette at home.*

—*Do you use screen time as a reward for your children or take screens away as a punishment? How often?*

—*Set a date to begin your own screen-free challenge. Decide whether you will start with one day per week, one week, two weeks, or longer.*

Chapter Seven

THE NEW ROUTINE

"Life happens in the interruptions." This simple motto has been transformative for me. I used to feel *so annoyed* whenever my kids interrupted my schedule and slowed down my checklist. For too long, I assumed that offering them screen time would guarantee that I could get something *done*. But relying on the screen time crutch *rarely* resulted in a feeling that I could get things done with the kids around.

C. S. Lewis said, "Children are not a distraction from more important work. They are the most important work." I had such a selfish attitude. What a shame to forget that they will only be children for a short time. I want to use what time that I have with my children wisely. I want to reprioritize how much time that I spend on entertainment and perceived productivity versus truly living. I want to multitask less and dedicate myself to one person or one task at a time. The following items are practical suggestions to take steps towards those goals.

Find quality moments with your child each day.

Perhaps you have so much on your plate that you often feel distracted during "quality time" with your child. Old habits die hard. Instead of multitasking or squeezing one "quick" task before you sit down with your child, put your child first, even if only for a moment. Take a moment to scoop up your child, look in her eyes, say, "I love you. Are you OK?" No matter your child's initial response, you are creating a loving foundation for your child. Then, if your task absolutely cannot wait, then explain that it is an emergency. But most of the time, the task *can* wait.

Instead of worrying about your to-do list, realize that you have a *unique opportunity* to interact *with your child*. A moment spent *fully present* and *undistracted* with your child is so much more worthwhile than a moment spent pulling your hair out because you never can keep up with the housework or emails or whatever else you wanted to attend to.

I've even found ways to treasure the morning rush. If I take one minute to hug the kids, ask them how they slept, and tell them that I love seeing them wake up in the morning, it's amazing how much more willing they are to listen to me when I inevitably ask, "Please finish up your breakfast . . . put your shoes on . . . get your backpack . . . go to the car." Take the initiative to connect with the kids first thing in the morning.

One of my favorite ways to make the most of a quick moment is to share a "20-second hug." Studies show that a 20-second hug from a loved one raises levels of the "love hormone" oxytocin, which "reduces levels of stress hormones (primarily cortisone) and decreases blood pressure in anxiety-producing events."[23] A big hug stimulates the nervous system, decreases loneliness, combats fear, raises self-esteem, alleviates tension, and communicates empathy.[24] So, hug for 20 seconds, read together for 5 minutes, play together for an hour. No matter the amount of time, highly prioritize quality time with your child each day!

Give your children the "gift of boredom."

I'd like to highlight Dr. Sigman's quote once again: "One of the greatest gifts that we can offer our children is the gift of boredom."[25] Remember that you are not merely *taking away* screens from your children, but you are *giving* them something in its stead: the ability to be content with less, to learn how to explore, learn, and discover all on their own.

Once you have had quality time with your child, then also set aside time in your children's schedule to do nothing in particular. Give them an opportunity to come up with an activity on their own. Children need free play. Pediatric research shows a direct relationship between the rise of anxiety and depression and the decline in free play.[26] Resist the urge to schedule every minute of your child's day. Allow them some freedom to just be kids.

Repeat after me: *Less is more.*

In this book, I mainly focus on the benefits of less screen time in a home. However, there are all kinds of traps that families fall into: parents working too much, families eating too much unhealthy food, kids overscheduled, and homes filled with too much *stuff*. The excess in our culture encourages that "entertain me" attitude. (i.e. Why *does* my child get a new plastic toy with every kids' meal? Why *are* my children automatically offered crayons, balloons, and cookies while we're grocery shopping or sitting at a restaurant?)

If your children are like mine, they have more than enough to do and more than enough to play with. The problem is that *they don't truly appreciate it.* A defining characteristic of restlessness is the inability to thoroughly enjoy things, the inability to be content with what one has. If you're like me, you may feel a twinge of guilt that you're taking away your children's beloved screen time. You may even be tempted to give them *more* things to play with and *more* special activities to do. At least, that's what I did at first. Believe me that it only causes a redirection of obsession and discontentment.

There is no reason to feel guilty about getting to the heart of your child's restlessness. Have confidence in limiting screen time *as well as all of those other things*. One of the biggest obstacles to restfulness is over-stimulation due to excess, whether it is too many screens, toys, junk foods, activities, you name it. Remove those obstacles for your child. Consider what you are giving to your child by taking away glut. Create a peaceful, minimal, healthy environment for your children to enjoy.

This brings me to my next recommendation.

While you're at it, take away all of their toys, too.

OK, bear with me here. I think that *excess stuff* deserves a category all its own. Dr. Sigman explains, "It has recently been found that reducing the number of toys children have has significant intellectual benefits. Too much variety distracts and confuses. Reducing the amount and intensity of stimulation we consume is one of the greatest challenges and achievements we could embark on."[27]

Did you read about the mom who reached a breaking point with her daughters' stuff around the house and very suddenly, and very literally took away *all* of their toys? She even stripped the girls' beds of their frilly comforters. The mom is a popular blogger and received all kinds of responses about her posting about that day. While I doubt her methods, I agree with her motivation. She writes, "I equated giving [my children] stuff with making them happy: a message that our consumer-driven cultures hammers into our psyches from the time that we are born. What a lie!"[28] A year later, she maintains that her daughters are happier, more content, no longer overwhelmed by piles of toys, and are able to discern excess around them in the world.

Instead of waiting until *your* breaking point with messes, start sorting it out *with* them. There are three options for clutter: toss, donate, or hide. Don't leave anything lying around, otherwise, those things will become unappreciated. Give your children fewer options so that they can appreciate what they have. And, yes, it may take longer to organize everything with their "help," but it's important that they are a part of the process.

Toss it.
If an old toy is outdated in safety standards or beyond repair, don't hesitate to toss it. Avoid the temptation to completely toss toys while your children aren't looking. Simply explain to them that broken things are not good to play with and should be thrown away.

Donate it.
Create a family donation box and start a conversation with your child about getting rid of things that the family no longer uses. First, have her help you clean out *your* closet. Explain that it is good to share, that others can enjoy things that we no longer need.

Then, encourage your child to donate some of her things. She may not choose to get rid of anything the first time that you suggest it. But, in starting an ongoing conversation, you are demonstrating respect for your child and her belongings, and you are encouraging her to start thinking about *quality over quantity*. A generous attitude is in stark contrast to an "entertain me" mindset.

Hide Everything Else.
Explain to the kids that there are too many things out. For example, I tell my kids, "We should find hiding spots for everything so that it will feel nicer in here. Did you know that toys like to live in their homes? Remember to take toys back to their home when we are finished playing."

So, create "homes" for their things: a drawer for puzzles, a cabinet for games, containers for Lego, a basket for balls, shelves for books, a box for stuffed animals. Make sure the kids understand where to find things so that they can remember where they belong. Otherwise, how can they be expected to clean up properly when the time comes?

If you keep the majority of the items that you start with, then the bins may be overflowing, books jammed into shelves, and drawers overstuffed. Show the kids that toys are not happy if we smash them into their homes. Help them see that an overfilled bin is an indication that some things should be donated.

Go to the library often.
While transitioning the kids away from screen time and excess, my saving grace was the library. The kids *love* to visit our little local library. The staff is enthusiastic and helpful, and of course, there is a wealth of quality books.

One of the things that I love most about our library is that there is only *one* computer in the children's section. It is a little slow on the uptake, and there is an automated time limit. So, while the kids initially complained about this feature, they got used to it. After getting to know where some of their favorite books were kept, that little computer lost its luster.

Two years ago, before we moved to the house where we now live, we used to go to a bigger, newer, and fancier library. It included several elaborate kids sections with a dozen computers, complete with dividers and individual headphones. I didn't see any children who were interested in checking out books. It's like, why choose a healthy snack when all of these candy bars are available?

So, choose your library wisely and visit often. Our library has helped me teach the kids that it's fun to borrow, take turns, and give back when we are finished with items. The very way that libraries function demonstrates the beauty of sharing and discovering.

Analyze your home's feng shui.

Consider whether the TV is the first thing seen when you walk in the door. Nowadays, houses are designed around screens. Modern houses feature TV cut-outs or ledges above the living room mantle with cable readiness—so that the room's focal point will be the TV. In our current house, we disabled wiring and sheet-rocked over a three-foot deep TV hole above the mantle. (Our house was built in 2005: before flat screen TVs!) We now enjoy a grouping of Jamie's paintings there, and we hide our TV in an armoire.

Rearranging just one or two spots around the house can naturally steer attention away from screens and towards creative activities. So, hide the TV in a cabinet. Keep the desktop computer screen turned off. Put the tablet in a drawer. Tuck away the laptop and the portable DVD player. *Above all,* as the AAP recommends,[29] be sure to remove all screens from your child's bedroom.

In other words, relocate all screens to inconvenient places out of reach, and reserve portable screens for specific tasks or long trips. At this point, all screens and all excess should be out of sight and out of mind, creating physical and mental space for everyone to feel more at ease and content.

Re-think your schedule.

Pinpoint the moments in day when your children typically ask for screen time, and insert a new activity during that time. The idea is to distract them from their routine of acting on restlessness.

For example, Isaiah would typically expect screen time as soon as he arrived home from school. So, I started avoiding going directly home after carpool. Instead, we would head to the library, the park, the store, maybe even go out for a popsicle. If and when Isaiah asked about screens upon finally arriving home, I would explain that we didn't have time for it. Maybe it was time for free play or decluttering time. Not every moment needs to be filled and dictated, right?

Dinner time was another trying time for our family regarding screen obsession. We rarely if ever had the TV on during dinner; however, I was concerned about how much screens dominated dinner conversation. For example, the kids would ask if they could have screen time after dinner, or they would talk about the latest favorite show, video game, or app. So, we started a new routine of taking time as a family to discuss our favorite part of the day and what each of us are thankful for that day. Encourage gratefulness to overshadow selfishness.

Encourage your child to be a "helper" every single day.

Another basic way to stave off a selfish or "entertain me" mentality is to encourage kids to "be a helper." Kids love to help, so let them. Every day. After all, they will have all of this new time on their hands because they are no longer in front of screens, right? That means that they will have all the more time to pitch in with chores!

If your kids dread hearing the word "chores," then rephrase it. Explain to your older children that taking care of your home is a *privilege*, not merely a *chore*. Tell your younger children that they are a helper, and maybe even make a game out of it.

One of the kids' favorite activities is, what we call, "the sock game!" Making chores enjoyable is all in the delivery. We have a special bucket for clean, unmatched socks. (OK, so it is actually a *regular* bucket that we happen to *say* is special.) First, Isaiah dumps it out on top of his head, and Ellie tosses socks into the air as if they are a pile of leaves in the fall. But even a toddler can match socks, and a five-year-old can fold them.

Of course, they *won't* be very efficient. It *will* take longer for you to get things cleaned up with the kids involved. You *could* get it done so much faster cleaning up by yourself or hiring someone to do it. But what would that communicate to your child?

There's no need to rush through clean-up time. There's no screen time at the end of it as a "reward." The time of enjoyment is *during* clean-up! It's spending time together while accomplishing a task. It's about making memories, working together, and learning to help. So, let the kids use the hand-held vacuum, toss things into the recycle bin, set the table, tuck in their chairs, clear the table, put silverware into the dishwasher, scrub the toilet, sort piles of laundry. Have a seat on the bathroom floor while they use scrubber brushes and sponges just for the fun of it. No matter what particular chore you choose, always ask them with kindness. At the end of each task, thank them for their help. They will feel wanted, appreciated, and proud of themselves for helping.

Carefully and intentionally acquire items in your home for learning and discovery.

So, you want to cut out screen time and excess stuff, and you want to foster a grateful and helping attitude in your children. Next, consider how your family spends time and money. What items fill the rooms in your home and command attention? Do you shop impulsively? How do you decide what does and doesn't belong in your home?

Specifically for your kids, consider that the items in your home have a subtle impact on their learning development. How can the items that you choose to have in your home encourage discovery and learning? What activities are your children naturally drawn to? What educational areas do you want to encourage your child to build interest in? Here are a few suggestions for items with educational purposes.

Science

Get young kids a play doctor kit; older kids, science sets. Look up easy experiments that you can do together at home. Place a basket by the back door with bug cages, buckets, shoes, and sunscreen for impromptu outdoor adventures. Before going screen-free, I used to slightly dread backyard time with the kids, because they would drag out so many things with them. Now, they are happy with rocks, leaves, and a pile of pine straw, and I am happy to send them outside.

Collect a few maps, find an old-fashioned globe, or do geography puzzles together. Hang scientific posters in the kids' playroom. For example, Isaiah was recently given a poster when we visited the local park. The poster illustrates plants and animals found in wetlands, and he can now identify poison ivy.

Art
If you haven't already, designate an art corner in your home, and give it some love. Before going screen-free, our art table was underutilized because of clutter. Get the kids to help organize. Put crayons in their place, and recycle coloring books that are used up. Buy a couple of new coloring books if you want, but a neat stack of blank paper and a box of crayons that you already have lying around go a long way.

Music
Designate a bin for kid-friendly instruments like shakers, whistles, rhythm sticks, harmonicas, drums, bells, etc. Or just put a handful of buttons in a plastic container, and you've made a shaker. Young children enjoy participating in music by moving, so include some scarves or flowing fabric for dancing.

Consider buying an acoustic piano or guitar, even if you don't play. Not enough room? Make room! Or maybe just consider smaller, digital versions of instruments instead.

Last year, I was excited to purchase a piano for my home, but I did not anticipate the extent that the entire family would enjoy it. It demands a lot of space in our little sunroom by the kitchen, so it gets a lot of loving attention. The kids enjoy exploring the mechanics, and they come up with their own musical creations.

Reading
A cozy blanket and library books are all you need for a reading "nook." A pillow and a tiny reading light make it even better. Keep it simple. Read enthusiastically and

often with your child. Check out books on CD from the library.

Writing
At the art table, offer the kids a small stack of blank cards, envelopes, and stickers for "stamps" to encourage letter writing and thank you notes. Isaiah, for example, has never much been interested in handwriting unless it had a specific purpose, such as writing a letter or a fun story. Only now that he is well into kindergarten has he shown interest in writing for its own sake. Having the writing materials handy has been a great help.

Listening
Listening is usually not an official subject in school, but Julian Treasure argues that it should be in his TED Talk, "Five Ways to Listen Better."

> We're becoming impatient . . . we want sound bites . . . the art of conversation is being replaced—dangerously, I think—by personal broadcasting . . . We're becoming desensitized. Our media have to scream at us with these kinds of headlines in order to get our attention, and that means it's harder for us to pay attention to the quiet, the subtle, the understated . . . Listening is our access to understanding . . . Why is listening not taught in schools? It is crazy.[30]

Mr. Treasure goes on to describe ways that people can practice listening more effectively. I have noticed in my own life that when I make a conscious effort to truly listen, conversations are so much more effective and meaningful. The way that our culture is, active listening takes effort and practice.

Help teach your children how to actively listen, give them time to practice. In the car, ask them what sounds they hear as you drive together. Make a game of closing your eyes for one minute and talking about what you hear when the timer goes off. Play telephone.

In general music education classes that I teach, I typically set aside a few minutes for the kids to close their eyes and listen to music. They are to decide what sounds are used as well as what mood is being communicated. For example, I ask, "What kinds of instruments or voices did you hear? Does this piece make you feel like dancing? Does it sound sad? Silly? Mysterious?" Even young children love to learn how to listen and summarize what they hear.

We recently acquired Jamie's parents' old record player and a stack of albums. Like our piano, it takes up a lot of room and is a centerpiece of the living room. The kids are fascinated by how it works. But if a record player isn't realistic for your family, then perhaps buy some MP3s, burn a few CDs (a child-friendly copy of music you have purchased), and set up an old boom box that your child can use on his own. When a CD gets scratched (and it will), just burn another one.

Physical Activity

One indication of restlessness that I've mentioned is fidgeting. Fidgeting is not only a huge obstacle to a child's ability to listen, but it is also an indication that a child is not getting enough exercise. We need to make sure that our kids are getting enough movement throughout the day, every day. Angela Hanscom, pediatric occupational therapist and founder of TimberNook (timbernook.com), "an innovative nature-based developmental program designed to foster creativity, imagination, and independent play in the great outdoors," puts it this way:

Many children are walking around with an under-developed vestibular (balance) system today due to restricted movement. In order to develop a strong balance system, children need to move their body in all directions for hours at a time... Fidgeting is a *real* problem. It is a strong indicator that children are not getting enough movement throughout the day. We need to fix the underlying issue. Recess times need to be extended and kids should be playing outside as soon as they get home from school. Twenty minutes of movement a day is not enough! They need hours of play outdoors in order to establish a healthy sensory system and to support higher-level attention and learning in the classroom. In order for children to learn, they need to be able to pay attention. In order to pay attention, we need to let them move.[31]

So, yes, sign them up for soccer and dance class, but realize that once- or twice-a-week structured activities is not enough. Send them outside to play hide-and-seek or freeze tag. They should be rolling, crawling, spinning, jumping, wiggling, running, and being wild. Encourage them to make up games based on favorite stories. Have a dance party, build a fort, go on a pretend camping trip in the basement. Hey, maybe even go on a real camping trip. Clean off that neglected trampoline or treehouse in the backyard. Go to the park, go on a hike, a walk around the neighborhood. The possibilities are endless. Just make sure your kids are moving, a lot, every day.

Handicrafts

My kids are fortunate enough to attend a Charlotte Mason school where handicrafts is an actual subject of study for all ages. The ability to create with our own two hands is a valuable experience for children.

For younger children, fill a bin with fabrics, glue, string, safety scissors, popsicle sticks, paper plates, pompoms, googly eyes, pipe cleaners, socks, etc. Help them make puppets, put on shows, make gifts, create small toys. Designate an air-tight container for play-dough—include plasticware, bowls, plates, small rolling pins, and other tools.

Give older children opportunities to learn how to sew, use a screwdriver, a tape measure, a gardening spade, a rolling pin. Do you know how much kids love to break eggs? It will absolutely make their day.

Pace Yourself

Strike a balance for activities that are easy for you to supervise and activities that the kids enjoy doing. Maybe you cringe at the thought of trying to cook alongside your child or teach him how to use scissors just yet. For me, it's watercolor. My kids love to paint, but I feel like I have to help them with every stroke in order to avoid complete chaos. For me, the energy that I expend is not worth the mess it creates. So, unless I have time for an extended period of quality time with the kids, I have learned to say, "No, we're not going to paint right now, but here's some washable markers."

Absolutely resist the temptation to be Super Parent, coming up with crazy and complicated activities at all times, day in and day out. That attitude will only fuel your children's desire to be entertained all the more. Always remember: *less is more, boredom is a gift, a little quality time goes a long way.* They *can* learn to be content without screens, and they *can* learn to entertain themselves for longer than you can imagine. Hang in there.

—Do you tend to multitask or often feel that the kids interrupt what you're doing? What seemingly important tasks can wait?

—What is your favorite way to spend quality time with your children?

—Do your children have free play every day? How can you offer them the gift of boredom?

—In what ways can your family cut out excess? How can your family practice the idea that less is more?

—Is your TV at the front and center in your home? Do your children have screens in their bedrooms?

—When are your children most likely to ask for screen time?

—Do you expect your children to be helpers every day? What responsibilities could you start teaching your children?

—What areas of learning do you hope to encourage in your children at home?

Chapter Eight

THE FREEDOM

For too long, I assumed that living screen-free would be a ridiculous and unbearable *constraint*. But when I reluctantly, finally gave it a chance, I found out that it is a wonderful and *liberating* way of living. On a purely surface level, it can be so refreshing: no more kids' apps on my phone, no more tablet games, no more setting a timer for computer games, no more loud kids' movies, no more annoying kids' TV shows, no more mind-numbing video games. There is less whining, more contentment; less stuff, more restfulness. But how can I be sure that the positive changes will last?

Spiritually Speaking

In Chapter Two, I mentioned that *our very nature stands in the way of contentment and true rest.* As a Christian, this concept resonates with me in a very real sense. Romans 3:23 says, "For all have sinned and fallen short of the glory of God." The Bible teaches that apart from God, all of mankind is unsatisfied and naturally pulled in unhealthy directions.

However, Jesus says in Matthew 11:28–30, "Come to me, all who labor and are heavy laden, and I will give you rest. Take my yoke upon you, and learn from me, for I am gentle and lowly of heart, and you will find rest for your souls. For my yoke is easy and my burden is light." I have found this to be absolutely true, and I am thankful for God's forgiveness and grace in my life.

Underlying Motivations and Heart Change

As a Christian parent, I should not only consider how my family spends its time, energy, and finances, but also consider what is taking up space in my heart. As I've mentioned before, Jamie and I initially made the decision to go screen-free mainly because I was at my wits' end. I just wanted to stop all of the restlessness, and finally, I was willing to try anything.

I see now that my initial motivation was essentially serving an idol of *a more peaceful home*. I wanted my kids to behave better; I wanted my house to be nice and neat; I wanted to feel like I could accomplish a task without being continually interrupted. I wanted to be independent. I was prideful.

It didn't take long for the kids to shift their addictions away from screens and onto new things. Only then did I realize the error of my initial motivation. In repentance, I confessed that I would be unable to truly help my children unless I ultimately pointed them to their need for God. Screens do not satisfy; new things do not satisfy. Psalm 145:16 says, "You open your hand; you satisfy every living thing." Only God can satisfy.

So, as you teach your children the value of "being a helper," go on to explain that we can honor God by taking care of what He provides for us. Yes, distract your children from their old way of life with new routines. Discourage their natural "entertain me" mentality by demonstrating selflessness and gratefulness. Listen to music together, read together, sit in the backyard and take note of the living things around you. But be sure to do all of these things in order to teach them to appreciate *God's creation*, to meditate on *God's goodness*, and to find moments of *true worship*.

"Teach Them Diligently"
Deuteronomy 6:4–7 says:

> Hear, O Israel, the Lord our God, the Lord is One. You shall love the Lord your God with all your heart and with all your soul and with all your might. And these words that I command you today shall be on your heart. You shall teach them diligently to your children, and shall talk of them when you sit in your house, and when you walk by the way, when you lie down, and when you rise. You shall bind them as a sign on your hand, and they shall be as frontlets between your eyes. You shall write them on the doorposts of your house and on your gate.

I have found it impossible to teach my children Scripture "diligently" if I do not set aside a specific time in the day to do so. Lord-willing, I also study Scripture and speak about it spontaneously with my children throughout the day. But I also see the benefit of choosing a designated time to talk about Scripture with my family each day.

Don't assume that your children will not be interested. It's OK if they don't perfectly understand when you talk about spiritual things. Don't be discouraged if their initial reaction is less than enthusiastic. Teaching Scripture to our children is something that we are commanded to do. It's important that we open the door to conversation about spiritual things early and often.

For our family, these Scripture discussions take place at dinner time. We challenge each other to memorize Scripture and talk about what it means to us. Even Ellie has memorized John 3:16 and snippets of other verses. One of my favorite passages that we memorized during our transition phase was Philippians 2:14, "Do all things without grumbling or questioning." Model a positive attitude about your new routine, and it will catch on. Before you know it, your children will be reminding *you* at dinner: "Mama, we forgot to do our verse!"

Simply having an ongoing activity to do together creates a bond with you and your children. My mom's favorite verse is Psalm 37:4, "Delight yourself in the Lord, and He will give you the desires of your heart." As I was teaching this to the kids, I was having them try to repeat it back.

I began: "Delight yourself—"

Isaiah continued, "—in the Lord—"

"—and he will give you the—"

"—*diseases* of your heart?"

We all burst into laughter, and we all love to retell that story.

Resting in God

We, as Christian parents, can rest in God by trusting Him in each moment, finding opportunities for worship in daily tasks, and sharing Scripture with our children. Children can rest in God simply by *being children*—by exploring, playing, eating, sleeping, laughing. Lord willing, they will grow in their knowledge of Scripture, pray, and accept God's grace in their lives. As much as it is our responsibility to provide for our children's physical well-being, it is also our responsibility to encourage their spiritual growth—by disciplining with kindness, by modeling grace, by teaching them Scripture. Always let your motivation be giving God glory and taking the best care of your family that you know how, one step at a time, one decision at a time, one moment at a time.

***

—*What is your underlying motivation to fight restlessness in your home? What is your motivation to unplug?*

—*At what time during your daily routine could you set aside time to teach Scripture to your children?*

—*As you embark on this new journey of cutting out screens in your home, jot down signs of progress and celebrate together.*

ACKNOWLEDGEMENTS

Endless thanks to **Jamie, Isaiah, and Ellie** for your patient love and support. What a joy to be a family together! **Mom & Dad**, thanks for always being my biggest supporters. **Tracy**, thank you for encouraging me to write out my story. Thanks for sharing articles with me and scheduling FaceTime conversations. Much love always to you and Aaron. **Melissa**, thank you for all of your suggestions. This book would truly be a mess without your help. **Nikki**, thank you for your listening ear, for helping me find the right feel for the cover design, and for creating the perfect illustrations for the cover. **Nancy**, thank you for your magical red pen and being my patient proofreader. What a labor of love! **Heidi**, thank you for all of your encouragement. It is a joy to be on staff at CDF. **Joel**, we Harpers are so thankful for you and Lauren and the girls being in our lives for all these years, and now getting to be neighbors. **Collin**, I'm so thankful for yours and Lauren's love and support. **Aric**, thank you so much for taking the time to call me from across the pond to encourage me in my endeavor. What a fun chat. You are an inspiration! **Ginger**, thank you for your encouragement. Hands-down, your book *Don't Make me Count to Three!* is my go-to for parenting help.

Portrait by Chris Garrison 2014

Tamara McLeod Harper lives in Birmingham, Alabama, with her family. She graduated from Birmingham-Southern College with a Bachelor of Arts in music. She teaches private music lessons out of her home and general music at Crestwood Day School. She is an accompanist at Children's Dance Foundation. You can find the Harpers' children's book, *Bird Alphabet,* on blurb.com/bookstore.

For book updates, visit www.livingrestfully.com.

ENDNOTES

[1] huffingtonpost.com/cris-rowan/10-reasons-why-handheld-devices-should-be-banned_b_4899218.html

[2] http://www.screenfree.org/wp-content/uploads/2014/01/screentimefs.pdf

[3] http://www.screenfree.org/research-and-fact-sheets/

[4] http://dharmaseed.org/teacher/360/talk/24014/

[5] Cutting, J. E., DeLong, J. E., Brunick, K. L., Iricinschi, C. I., and Candan, http://www.academia.edu/610807/Quicker_Faster_Darker_Changes_in_Hollywood_Film_Over_75_Years

[6] Sigman, Aric. "Well Connected?" *The Biologist* Vol 59 No 1 (2009): 15

[7] http://newsroom.ucla.edu/releases/in-our-digital-world-are-young-people-losing-the-ability-to-read-emotions

[8] www.philly.com/philly/blogs/healthy_kids/THe-AAP-issues-new-media.html?c=r

[9] http://pediatrics.aappublications.org/content/132/5/958.full

[10] http://pediatrics.aappublications.org/content/132/5/958.full

[11] Bilton, Nick. "Steve Jobs Was a Low Tech Parent." *The New York Times,* Sept 11, 2014. http://www.nytimes.com/2014/09/11/fashion/steve-jobs-apple-was-a-low-tech-parent.html?_r=0

[12] Barr, Leticia. "Teaching Digital Safety to All Ages." *Tech Savvy Mama.* TechSavvyMama.com, 20 June 2014

[13] http://www.cox.com/aboutus/takecharge/tween-internet-safety-survey/10-tips-for-parents.cox?campcode=takecharge_about-std-promo_about-takecharge_0612

[14] Bilton, Nick. "Steve Jobs Was a Low Tech Parent." *The New York Times,* Sept 11, 2014. http://www.nytimes.com/2014/09/11/fashion/steve-jobs-apple-was-a-low-tech-parent.html?_r=0

[15] "Media and Children." *American Academy of Pediatrics.* https://www.aap.org/en-us/advocacy-and-policy/aap-health-initiatives/pages/media-and-children.aspx

[16] Richtel, Matt. "A Silicon Valley School That Doesn't Compute." *The New York Times,* October 22, 2011. http://www.nytimes.com/2011/10/23/technology/at-waldorf-school-in-silicon-valley-technology-can-wait.html?pagewanted=all/&_r=1

[17] Ginsburg, Kenneth R. "The Importance of Play in Promoting Healthy Child Development and Maintaining Strong Parent-Child Bonds." *American Academy of Pediatrics.* http://www2.aap.org/pressroom/playfinal.pdf

[18] http://www.contentedbaby.com/books-AricSigmanInterview.html

[19] http://whole30.com/whole30-program-rules/

[20] http://www.contentedbaby.com/DawnFozard_Television.htm

[21] http://www.metroparent.com/core/pagetools.php?pageid=17022&url=%2FMetro-Parent%2FMay-2014%2FFamilies-Unplug-for-One-Week-in-Screen-Free-Challenge%2Findex.php&mode=print

[22] www.simplicityparenting.com/screen-free-week-confessions/ http://seedlingsnurseryschoolaz.blogspot.com/2013/04/screen-free-week-2012-recap.html

[23] Dr. Mercola. "Fun Facts About Hugging." *Mercola.com*, February 6, 2014. http://articles.mercola.com/sites/articles/archive/2014/02/06/hugging.aspx

[24] http://happinessweekly.org/2013/01/19/fun-facts-about-hugging/

[25] http://www.mumsnet.com/qanda/aric-sigman

[26] www.psychologytoday.com/blog/freedom-learn/201001/the-decline-play-and-rise-in-childrens-mental-disorders

[27] http://www.contentedbaby.com/books-AricSigmanInterview.html

[28] http://www.livingwellspendingless.com/2012/09/14/why-i-took-all-my-kids-toys-away-why-they-wont-get-them-back/

[29] http://www.aap.org/en-us/advocacy-and-policy/aap-health-initiatives/Pages/Media-and-Children.aspx

[30] www.ted.com/talks/julian_treasure_5_ways_to_listen_better/transcript?language=en

[31] http://www.balancedandbarefoot.com/blog/the-real-reason-why-children-fidget

Made in the USA
Charleston, SC
05 April 2015